Dealing with Depositions

Tips for Healthcare Professionals

Steven Oscherwitz MD

ISBN: 979-8-9904736-0-7

Front cover image by Steven Oscherwitz, MD.

https://www.amazon.com/stores/author/B082YXSHTW/about?ingress=0&visitId=f8d9bcd7-1a12-4ee8-ad7e-42e044cad59e

An attorney friend once told me that "a doctor's job is to make black and white out of gray, and an attorney's job is to make gray out of black and white."

Over my subsequent decades in medical practice, I found that medical malpractice lawsuits certainly do seem to work that way. Events that might seem straightforward and logical to us do not always appear that way to others. Emotion and appearance may play overly large roles in a malpractice lawsuit, rather than just the facts and science that usually guide us in caring for our patients.

Each day, we place everything on the line to help our patients. One lawsuit exceeding the limits of our malpractice insurance policy could easily bankrupt us. Money saved over years of practice, residency, college and high school can be taken, and your spouse's savings might also be at risk in community property states. "Jane Doe Oscherwitz" is always intentionally named on the subpoenas that I receive.

Dealing with a lawsuit is certainly stressful, adding more work to our already busy schedules, straining our personal relationships and adversely affecting our self-perception.
The prolonged time course of the legal proceedings can make things even worse, since malpractice cases may take several years to resolve.

Each side retains separate experts to support their view of a case. Those experts may give the jury conflicting information and no clear right or wrong on a given injury. Going in front of a jury can be a gamble for that reason. Many frivolous or scientifically incorrect cases still make their way into our legal system, with their associated costs in time and money. Each malpractice case represents a risk to our well-being both during the legal proceedings and afterward.

Expert witnesses and plaintiffs attorneys are not too sympathetic, standing ready to profit from malpractice cases.

Even friends and family might not be too supportive; you must have done something terribly wrong to be involved in a lawsuit, right?

Many healthcare providers view all attorneys as the enemy, not realizing that this can work against them in a lawsuit. Attorneys defending us should always be viewed as partners, and we can assist in our own defense by providing our law team with accurate information in a timely fashion.

Your lawyer may not know all of the subtle details of your case, and you can help them fill in any knowledge gaps or let them know about special circumstances that might not be apparent to someone just looking at the chart or hearing the case for the first time.

If your medical malpractice insurance company assigns you a defense attorney, that individual will likely do a fine job. In cases where the stakes are high or with multiple defendants at odds with each other, however, you may need to also hire your own defense attorney at your own expense to assure that your interests are served.

You should promptly report any incidents that might have legal ramifications to your medical malpractice insurance company. The companies have telephone or online portals available to you for reporting cyberattacks, patient care occurrences, claims or lawsuits.
Any information that you provide about your exposure to liability now can assist the company in defending you later.

Risk management and general information hot lines provided by your malpractice insurer are good resources any time that you have questions, not just when a lawsuit is imminent.

Thorough documentation in your medical charts is also helpful, and critical to your successful defense later.
Never go back and change records when you are notified of a lawsuit. Original copies are likely already in adversarial hands, and altering the chart may cost you credibility and your case.

Once a lawsuit has been served, it is too late for "asset protection" schemes, and any subsequent transfers of assets might be reversed if you lose the case. Such attempts to hide assets make you look bad in court, and can enrage the plaintiff, the plaintiff's attorney and jury members.

The different events involved in a malpractice lawsuit are listed on the following pages, with some information about each for you.

SUBPOENA AND RECORD DISCLOSURE

Receiving notice of a lawsuit at your home or office is certainly one of the most stressful situations you can face. Being served in a malpractice case is the first step of a difficult time in your life that may last for years. Your spouse may also be named in the lawsuit, since many healthcare providers put assets under their spouse's name or share community property with them.

Subpoenas are issued by the superior court in the county where the hearing or trial is to be held, and command your attendance at a deposition, hearing or trial. The initial subpoena may also include a command to produce documents, electronically stored information, tangible things or to permit the inspection of your office. The subpoena will state a date for delivering requested medical records and include a signed patient information release. In Arizona, the subpoena must be served at least 10 days prior to the requested delivery date for the patient's records. You can file a written objection if the above requirements are not met, or if you have other objections to providing the information.

Subpoenas for records typically request the records be delivered to the plaintiff's attorney's office.
A subpoena to bring records to trial will usually specify how to comply.

Do not ignore subpoenas. You should get in touch with your attorney immediately if you receive one. Any objections need to be made within 7 – 14 days of receipt, or you forever waive your right to object to any portion or all of the subpoena.

Subpoena objections may be made if the subpoena calls for disclosure of confidential, proprietary or sensitive information (i.e., trade secrets, business strategies or confidential customer information). Your attorney may elect to object to the subpoena and require that your confidential information be protected. Some subpoenas are quite broad, and may seem to call for hundreds or even thousands of documents. Your attorney can help you understand your obligations, and may be able to narrow the scope of the subpoena through negotiations.

Medical practitioners must ensure that written authorization to release the records has been obtained from the patient or their representative. You should develop a standard office procedure to assure compliance with patient record disclosure laws and avoid HIPAA violations.

You should not speak to anyone other than your attorney about the subpoena or the underlying lawsuit or investigation. You will be asked under oath later about your discussions regarding the case with individuals you know or persons at your company. Such conversations may come up later in a harmful way during depositions or trial.

Do not destroy or throw away documents which could possibly relate to the subpoena. Contact your IT department to turn off auto-deletion protocols on relevant email and other accounts to avoid court sanctions.

Any report that you give to your insurance company should be brief, using as few words as possible, without any admissions of guilt.
Any such communication is discoverable by a plaintiff's attorney.

Only discussions with your lawyer are 100% protected from disclosure.
(However, your attorney will be reporting case details to your malpractice insurance carrier. You must be specific about any details that you do not want shared).

DEPOSITION

Deposition definition and details:

- An out of court examination of a witness or party under oath

- Taken to gather information and preserve testimony

- Testimony is recorded and transcribed by a court reporter (in question and answer form). Audio and video recordings are also kept in some cases, in addition to the transcript document.

- No judge or jury is present.

- Witnesses may be compelled to attend depositions by subpoena.

- Any portion of a deposition transcript can be used in a trial.

- The deposition transcript may be used to undermine the credibility of a witness who responds to questions with unreliable, biased, inconsistent or false statements.

You should notify your malpractice insurance carrier any time that you are contacted about giving a deposition, and your carrier should pay for an attorney to defend you.

It is a good idea to have your attorney present at your deposition. All depositions are significant. You may become involved in litigation any time you give testimony under oath, and your rights need be protected.

Make sure to choose a neutral location for your deposition. Ideally, the deposition should take place in your attorney's office or at a court reporter's office, rather than in your own office. This prevents interruptions so that you can focus on the disputed case. Also, items that you have in your office could attract the plaintiff attorney's attention and later be used against you (patient handouts, outdated textbooks, etc.). Conducting the deposition at your attorney's office also makes it more difficult for the patient's attorney to request additional records or documents from you during the deposition.

Deposition preparation is VERY important, especially if you will be appearing on videotape. Have your attorney request your malpractice carrier pay for a full day or more of professional preparation. It is expensive and time consuming, but absolutely worth it. Facing tough questions before the deposition can be very helpful, allowing you to think carefully about how you will answer them. A full critique should follow, allowing you to find effective / persuasive ways to accurately answer questions. This type of dress rehearsal is protected by attorney-client privilege.

Doing research ahead of a deposition may not be in your best interest. When it is done, the plaintiff's attorney will want to know what references you reviewed and look at those in order to get ammunition to use against you. Questioning about "how you didn't bother to look it up when treating the patient, but did so only to protect yourself in the lawsuit," may also come up.

Plaintiff's lawyers and their nurse paralegals will go over medical records in great detail, looking for ways to surprise and trap you. You should know every detail of your case records so you will be able to fend off such attacks, and this will take a lot of time for both you and your attorney.

All of the information revealed at your deposition will not necessarily be admissible in court.

PREPARING FOR A DEPOSITION

- Review the case in detail with your attorney.

- Assist your attorney in understanding the relevant medical terminology, procedures and technology of your case.

- Make sure that you understand your legal team's litigation and deposition strategies.

- Review your medical records as well as any documents, reports or literature provided by your attorney in detail.

- Be prepared to explain the medical aspects of your case using terms easily understandable by lay persons. Realize that effective communication requires preparation. You must show patience, persistence and strong commitment to your patient's well-being.

DURING A DEPOSITION

During a deposition or testimony, responding slowly and clearly is important. Do not hurry to answer. You must think before speaking, even if the delay seems uncomfortable to you or others. Your pauses will not appear in the record later.

Having the medical record in front of you to refer to and using it as you answer makes sure that you state the facts correctly, and shows that you are thorough and know exactly what happened when the case unfolded many months or years ago. Your words are all transcribed and will carry much more weight if you use fewer words and avoid fillers like "um", "uh", "mm", "like" and "you know".

Excessive speech or volunteered information can be a problem, allowing an attorney to twist your words or encourage you to make statements that may be incriminating.

Your appearance, apparel and attitude are very important when you appear for any legal proceeding.
Your responses are videotaped or recorded for evaluation later by attorneys, judges and jurors during a trial. During a deposition, you are being tested for candor, honesty and courtroom demeanor to see how you might do if you appear later in front of a jury.

Poor behavior or a disheveled appearance at your depositions or trial can discredit you later. You should look professional in both demeanor and dress, be courteous and even-tempered.

Loss of composure or failure to take the proceeding seriously may be extremely harmful to your case.

Opposing lawyers know that your attitude and overall impression on a jury may be every bit as significant as your testimony. They will test, probe and attack all aspects of your courtroom presentation beginning at your deposition.

More tips for your deposition:

- Be honest and answer all questions truthfully.

- If a question is unclear, ask the attorney to repeat it, rephrase it or clarify it. **Make sure that you understand all questions, and do not answer questions that you do not understand.** Some questions asked may purposefully have terms with more than one meaning, while other questions are complex or lengthy on purpose.

- Avoid using phrases like

"I think…"
"I believe…"
"I am sure…"
"I assume…"
"Probably…"

- Avoid speculation or guessing. Say "I don't know," if you don't know something. You should make it clear to the examining lawyer that your answer is based only on an estimate, if that is the case.
Do not agree with statements by your questioning attorney that begin with "Would it be fair to say…"

- Do not volunteer information.
 Answer only the questions that you are asked, with as few words as possible. Yes or no answers are fine. "Educating" the examining lawyer is a bad idea, and is not your job.

- Wait to hear the entire question before answering.
 Misinterpretation is certainly a risk if you don't hear the entire sentence, and waiting gives your attorney a chance to object to improper questions. If the examining lawyer asks you to respond after your attorney objects, you should provide the

answer, unless your attorney instructs you otherwise.

- Have the patient's chart in front of you to refer to, or ask to see any relevant documents if there are questions about those. Do not rely on your memory alone.

- If you find that you have made a mistake, or a previous answer that you provided was incorrect, inform your lawyer.

- Ask for breaks, if you need them, especially if you become fatigued or uncomfortable. You can have your lawyer request a recess if you need to speak privately.

- During recesses, do not become conversational or relaxed with anyone except your own attorney. Keep your guard up, and speak with your attorney only in private, if that is necessary.

- Make sure that you stay alert until your deposition has been completed. The best lawyers save the most important questions for the end.

Depositions may go on for hours, and this can allow a plaintiff's attorney "wear down" a provider to the point that they will agree to anything or say anything to end the misery.
One trick that I have used to fight this over the years seems to work well.
The deposition meetings often begin at 9:00 or 10:00 AM, stop at about noon for lunch, and then resume about 1:00 or 2:00 PM. Before the deposition begins, I usually go get two cheeseburgers, french fries and a chocolate milkshake (or other calorie dense meal). When the plaintiff's attorney asks if everyone would like to break for lunch, I indicate that I would not (since I am still full from my meal earlier), and that I would like to finish the work without delay. Delaying or missing lunch

definitely irritates many plaintiff's attorneys and catches them off guard. They may subsequently become angry and say things to discredit themselves or their case on the record, especially if I remain composed and take my time thumbing through the chart and answering questions with minimal words.

- You have the right to review and correct your deposition transcript before you sign it.
An electronic or printed copy will usually be sent to you in the weeks after your deposition. Make sure that you read your deposition transcript closely when you receive it, correct any mistakes, and return it promptly to the issuing attorney.
Waiving your right to read and sign your deposition document is a mistake.

AFTER YOUR DEPOSITION

In your malpractice case, depositions will be taken from the patient, nurses, doctors, other involved medical personnel and medical experts. They may give their depositions before or after yours, and you will likely be asked to read through the transcripts of each one at some point. Make sure to let your attorney know exactly what you think of the other participants' deposition statements, including any errors that you feel are present in their testimony.

Counseling, including psychology or psychiatry assistance, may be helpful for you in dealing with the prolonged stress and demoralization that go with being sued. You may benefit from such interventions, even if your family and friends are supportive.

A court date will be set for your case to be heard in front of a judge and jury. That date may seem far off initially.

As the facts of your case become more clear, plaintiff and defendant attorneys will often seek to settle the case for a sum of money before that court date, avoiding your appearance at trial before a jury. You will be asked to approve such a settlement, if that occurs.

The settlement amount will hopefully be covered by your malpractice insurance, but in the worst cases, the plaintiff team may seek more than your insurance covers, and you might be at risk for significant personal losses or even bankruptcy.

In such a case, the attorney assigned to you by your medical malpractice insurance company might be instructed by that company to manage the case in a way to minimize their losses. That might not always be in your best interest.

In cases where the stakes are high or with multiple defendants at odds with each other, you may need to hire your own defense attorney at your own expense to assure that your interests are served.

Hiring your own attorney usually involves hiring "personal counsel" to advise and act on your behalf without being the counsel of record.

It would be prohibitively expensive to pay your own attorney to completely take over the case, and malpractice insurance company "cooperation clauses" give them the right to assign the lawyers who actually work on your case as counsel of record.

SETTLEMENT

In past years, a $1 million malpractice insurance policy was sufficient protection for providers, with plaintiffs settling for that amount unless the injury was especially bad or the defendant's conduct outrageous.

This is no longer the case, and any wrongful death or severe injury case is potentially worth more than $1 million in front of a jury.

Mega salaries for sports stars have desensitized jurors to big numbers, and jurors assume that all doctors and other healthcare providers have multiple millions of dollars of insurance coverage.

Additionally, plaintiff's attorneys may hire what is called a "future cost of a life-care plan witness" for their malpractice cases.

These witnesses make huge estimates for future care costs that ignore insurance, government programs and other assistance.

It is a cottage industry, rolling out 7 and 8 figure damage estimates.

Juries don't usually award 100 cents on the dollar for these, but such a situation can be a financial sword of Damocles hanging over a provider who has only a $1-2 million malpractice insurance policy.

Employed healthcare providers should also understand that if they work for a big group or hospital, they typically don't have the right to give or withhold consent to settlement, as they would with an individual malpractice insurance policy.

The group or hospital makes that call, but it is usually the group or hospital that is on the financial hook if things go bad.

It is always wise to have a knowledgeable attorney review your employment contract to make sure that you are protected if both you and your group or hospital are sued.

If you are forced to settle defensible cases, you may have problems with your Medical Board, and have difficulty finding malpractice coverage later.

AFTER THE CASE

It will seem as though a huge weight has been lifted from your shoulders once your case is done and over. The constant worry about what might happen will be slowly replaced by a return to your usual routines and thoughts.

Protecting your assets from lawsuits using IRA accounts, a limited liability corporation or domestic asset protection trust should be a priority. Your estate planning lawyer and accountant can help you with these measures.

I always asked my defense attorneys for feedback about how I did after each case, and I was able to better defend myself the next time as a result of their suggestions. I eventually felt comfortable enough to assist some of those same lawyers in defending other doctors, nursing homes and hospitals from frivolous or misdirected medical lawsuits.

Whether you win or lose your case, the lessons that you learn during your time in the legal world won't be easily forgotten. You will certainly have a different perspective on your life, your work and your family afterwards. My hope is that these tips will help prepare you and make your case go more smoothly.

Good luck!